THE STONES ON THORPENESS BEACH

Also by Neil Powell from Carcanet

True Colours: New and Selected Poems

NEIL POWELL

THE STONES ON THORPENESS BEACH

CARCANET

First published in 1994 by
Carcanet Press Limited
208-212 Corn Exchange Buildings
Manchester M4 3BQ

Some of these poems originally appeared in
*Agenda, Critical Survey, London Magazine,
Outposts, PN Review, Poetry Review.*

A CIP catalogue record for this book
is available from the British Library.
ISBN 1 85754 058 1

The publisher acknowledges financial assistance
from the Arts Council of Great Britain.

Set in 10pt Joanna by Bryan Williamson, Frome
Printed and bound in England by SRP Ltd, Exeter

In memory of Adam Johnson
1965-1993

> Their understanding
> Begins to swell; and the approaching tide
> Will shortly fill the reasonable shore,
> That now lies foul and muddy.

Shakespeare: *The Tempest*

Contents

IV

I

For Music

It's a genuine sense of my own unworthiness
that's made me delay this thank-you letter for so long,
and still I feel nervous about beginning,
as if our steady affair is less

a relationship than a consequence of being –
born in misunderstanding, like all biographies –
or else an intrusion on family ties
too intimate and too far-reaching

for me to tangle with. Your shadier relatives,
encountered long ago, in strange and shady places,
mustn't be denied their proletarian graces
which may, after all, have shaped our lives:

like tough boys in the playground, whose threats were promises,
they tattooed their names on a child's imagination –
Paul Anka, Elvis Presley, Frankie Lymon
and (O brave new word!) The Teenagers –

so much packed in the emblems of a generation,
such confidence that we were the first who'd ever heard,
that soon we'd even swoon over Cliff Richard.
No doubt it's a shaming admission

if I confess I never liked the stuff but wanted
(as with film-stars, footballers) to have one of my own,
or get in on the act myself. Thus began
the world's worst pop group, and thus ended:

no harm in that, beyond embarrassment and broken
guitar-strings; as painless a way as we could manage
  to skid through adolescent rites of passage,
    though clearly it couldn't last. By then

I'd fallen for jazz, that potent echo of an age
just past, experience just missed, yet surviving
  for the dusty, smoky moment: hours browsing
    in Dobell's basement among vintage

78s, and enraptured evenings listening
to visiting Americans, Monk or Ellington
  playing 'Round Midnight' or 'In a Mellowtone'
    live in London – it don't mean a thing

if it ain't got that swing… Would you believe I even
wrote a monthly column for the *Daily Telegraph*
  as a 'Young Critic': took it on for a laugh,
    the records, and for Philip Larkin,

who did their proper jazz reviews and so chose my stuff –
a kindly, sad man I'm glad in the end to have met.
  Meanwhile, formed almost the world's worst jazz quartet,
    proved that devotion isn't enough,

despite Pee Wee Thornton on alto and clarinet
(the John Coltrane of Hunter's Hill), and two more cronies
  stretched past the limit of their abilities;
    Tirez (however) *le pianiste!*

You see, Music, I'd a simple trick to learn, which is:
work at your second love, and keep your first well-guarded;
  that's why I'm hunched over this sort of keyboard
    and not the illusive ivories.

I owe a surprising debt to Mr Collingwood,
who taught some odds and ends of English to the sixth form:
    one dozy afternoon in the autumn term,
        finding his class strangely depleted

by illness or excursion, he took the remnants home
to his flat across the High Street, bribed us with coffee,
    played a record of the Orchestral Suite in B
        minor by Bach. It worked like a charm,

works still (for heaven's sake): it's strange how momentously
the certainty struck that this was the stuff after all,
    and that it was almost inexhaustible,
        centuries of it stored up for me.

The road to Damascus? Well, nearly. Unlike St Paul,
what I'd tumbled to was addition, not conversion:
    for this was the mid-sixties, spinning on
        the kaleidoscopic musical

merry-go-round that drove the Beatles' revolution,
though it had hardly started. True, they'd topped the charts and
    even been taken seriously, had earned
        famous praise from the *Times*' William Mann

while delirious Beatlemania swept the land,
but so much of the best was still to come: *Revolver*;
    'Penny Lane' and 'Strawberry Fields Forever';
        Sgt Pepper's Lonely Hearts Club Band.

Thus some gullible critics began to consider
a grand reunion of your scattered family,
    including the freaks, all living happily
        in peace, brotherhood, etcetera;

so Maxwell Davies arranged McCartney's 'Yesterday'
(as if it needed it), and there was David Bedford
    hopping between the Soft Machine and the Third,
      and The Who with a piece called Tommy,

which they claimed was 'rock opera', and nobody laughed.
But meanwhile your poor relations were breeding again,
    poorer, meaner than ever, punkishly vain,
      leaving the sixties gratefully dead.

My formative Bach was pre-authentic: Menuhin
in boxy suites with the Bath Festival Orchestra,
    or with George Malcolm in the odd sonata;
        the Pears/King's College *St John Passion*;

and astonishing bargains – Harry Newstone's Saga
LPs of the *Brandenburgs*, Martin Galling's *Goldberg*
    Variations, ubiquitous Wurttemberg
        Chamber Orchestra, Segovia

and Rosalyn Tureck on a blurred ten-bob bootleg.
Sturdy eternal vinyl, they travelled beside me
    through nomadic student days to provide me
        with pleasure and a musical peg

to hang my ideals on when the world rocked too wildly.
Hence the harsh injunction to descend a semitone,
    to relish scrapes and scratches of a hard-won
        warts-and-all originality

didn't seem an unfettered blessing, nor was it one:
for Harnoncourt and Hogwood and Parrott and Pinnock
    (the latter in that ludicrous rustic smock)
        brought restoration, revelation,

heightened contrasts as a protecting veil was thrown back;
yet the result was uncomfortable, like living
    in a freshly spring-cleaned room, somehow wanting
        to turn down the contrast, smudge the black

and glacial white. I remember disagreeing
about not Bach but *Dido and Aeneas*, damned by
    choosing Janet Baker, not Emma Kirkby,
        unrepentant and unrepenting.

It's sad that certainties fell so unhelpfully
out of favour (on Radio 3 some smug buffoon
    just now said: 'No-one believes in the canon
        any more'), for self-evidently

Dido and Aeneas makes an excellent touchstone:
whichever way we cast our vote, we'll have to admit
    that our desert island must have room for it,
        and that uncommitted abstention

would be unforgivable. Music, it's your habit
to make us disputatious: think how passionately
    I'll argue the merits of Gerald Finzi,
        Samuel Barber, Michael Tippett,

the off-centre romantics true to our century;
or how ruthlessly deride my cranky aversions,
    Brahms, Chopin, Liszt. Such harmless diversions
        clutter the central issue, namely

you've provided some transmogrifying occasions –
the first encounters with Shostakovich or Britten
    or Mahler, composers who've somehow grown
        to become components, possessions,

bits of the inmost self. 'And if you could take just one?'
(whatever, you'd grow to loathe it, the question's crazy).
    Well, it has to be Mahler, it has to be
        Simon Rattle, his *Resurrection*.

Out here in East Anglia, we're in a sense lucky:
we've one of the loveliest concert halls in the land
    (though some of the dimmest audiences) and
        the power of chance or destiny

has blessed it. Between works, between August storms, to stand,
as liquid-patterned starlings flock above the reed-beds,
    against the dusk, as distant lightning recedes
        over the dark sea, and as inland

a clearing evening sky turns luminous blue and floods
the landscape with unearthly brilliance…this, Music,
    is beyond even your transforming magic,
        though comprehended in your concords.

But if that conceit's a shade Pythagorean, take
a different meshing of art and geography:
    in Britten I always hear the howling sea,
        its intermittent calm and sharp break

over the stony ridge; and it's there, obsessively,
not just in *Peter Grimes*, but a constant shifting ground
    (no paradox to those who live within sound
        of Aldeburgh beach); inevitably,

in the intricate transactions of tides, shingle, sand,
there's a music perpetually changing, renewing.
    So now, a disc of Pogorelich playing
        early Haydn, making it new-found,

as it always is and must be, nudges at something
we might have guessed all along: that to rediscover
    is the only true discovery, that our
        necessary task is remaking

the fractured past. In dislocated times, whenever
our lives are uncertain and our best words meaningless,
you nourish us with coherence and wholeness:
Music, may you flourish for ever.

The Black Bechstein

G.A.T., 1963

I was late on the scene.
Some timbers still smouldered,
Though most were dust by then
As, like the conclusion
Of a Victorian disaster
In industrial engineering,
The piano's skeleton uttered
Its final fractured notes
From random, cooling strings.

I was an adolescent,
Moved more by the occasion
Than what it meant. And yet,
A foolish schoolmaster,
Fellow-musician and thus
Not your favourite colleague
(All staffrooms are like that)
Thought I, your pupil, might best
Tell you the worst.

I found you in the garden.
I chatted casually.
You'd taught me this, for you'd
Begin each lesson that way,
Lowering the tension
Before a note was played.
I told you in your own
Calm tone: the music rooms;
Your Bechstein; all
Destroyed.
         You thanked me,
Went on digging quietly.

No other place or piano
Would do. You never forgave
The bringer of bad news,
And I could never forgive
Myself that self-importance,
The awful sense of occasion.
I'd be a pianist, if…

But there it was: we quarrelled –
Your lonely resentment
And my arrogant defences –
Until I walked out, leaving
You to contemplate
The callousness of children.

Borodins and Vodka

For Dmitri Shebalin

A resident quartet.
A form of words, and yet
Through catastrophic days
This bleak eroded coast
Provides, as it has done
Before, safe anchorage.
Resident: at worst
Administrative fiction;
At best, true habitation,
Huge vodkas in the Keys.

There's something in the air
Of Suffolk-Russian kinship:
How many programmes pair
Britten-Shostakovich.
And Ben's interpreters:
Richter, Rostropovich.
A chill from the sea, perhaps;
The windy never-stillness
Impels us to create
Our best, our better-than.

Evenings we'll not forget:
That January storm
Percussed the Maltings roof
(Tchaikovsky 3 beneath);
Fine Easter miniatures
Or Summer Russian masters
With family connections
In eloquent sonatas;
A form of words, and yet
A resident quartet.

II

The End of Summer

I close my eyes. There's a knotty apple-tree,
Grasped to a landscaped lawn, its fruit unripe;
A labrador, greying at the jowls, asleep;
My mother, gently stabbing at the crossword
With mild success; my father is at work.

I am at home now, but not for long.
My imagination is going to take me away.
Things are about to change: I've heard rumours,
Like odd creaks on the stairs, while I'm in bed
Fading in tune with Radio Luxembourg.

We've been to get my new school uniform
At the outfitters: a sombre narrow shop,
Innocent of daylight or fresh air,
With a sombre narrow man who peered at me
As if I wasn't quite their class of boy.

'Still in short trousers' means just what it says:
'Only rough boys wear jeans.' Long trousers now;
My mother sews in Cash's woven name-tapes
While I watch *Juke Box Jury*. Ding! A hit!
I've seen the future, and he's called Craig Douglas.

I pass whole days in an ecstasy of growing,
This wonderful summer: I empathise with plants –
Beans running, bamboo shooting, even the bees
Have somehow heard a buzz and are on the scent.
I know more than could possibly be good for me.

The stillness of held breath is on the air,
While thunder gathers in the wings of autumn.
I know high cloud will slowly bleach the sky,
Leaves turn to russet, late apples ripen,
And light will never be quite like this again.

Celandines

Some places stay for ever. Celandines
In bright rapacious grace beside the brook;
Mossed scent of earthy paths in bluebell woods;
Animal warmth of cloying straw-floored yards;
Deep meadows in their unwilled distances.

I'd play my game of hide-and-seek with life,
And win at every turn: they'd not catch me.
The garden-end and tunnelled undergrowth,
The roped and laddered oak – fine strategies
For a duke self-exiled from his childish court.

But hostile powers – Mynthurst, Stumblehole –
Defined themselves with cattle-grids or wires,
First iron curtains of the growing world:
The pebbled lane led on to tarmacked road,
Where bus-lamps shone in puddles after school.

Myself, I'd keep a life in walking distance,
Celandine-bright, mapped as a private planet.
In dreams, I'm in that other garden still:
Beyond the ditch, the fields remain unbounded,
But outer space begins at Norwood Hill.

Shell

I am schooled in the varieties of madness.
Feared beyond nickname, the Reverend dispensed
Lines for transcribing in copybook script,
Unflinching authority, Latin and caning
As if his future depended upon it.

Borrowed on odd days, like the pitches,
With crinkle-cut hair and sandpapered face,
The games-master cultivated his own pleasures.
'Posture!' he'd yell: frozen already, we'd freeze.
On the way back to school, he'd de-bag stragglers.

After two years, we trekked upstairs to 'Shell':
A whiskery, tweedy, leathery sort of place
With squeaky hinged seats, a tuckshop cupboard,
An air of dim complicity. From Mr Salmon,
I learned only to evade his hand-picked attention.

There are photos to prove it. In one I'm slouched
Like a doll who's yet to have stuffing knocked in;
But later – I'm standing now, behind the Reverend –
There's that horrible confident smirk of survival:
I'd known most of the worst of the world by ten.

Old fools, the lot of them, not even doing
A quarter of their best, not caring or seeing
How much there was to give or how to give it;
Teaching instead bad habits by default –
Slow lessons in obsession, terror, guilt.

Sixpence for the Man

Two silver coins in penny-farthing scale:
'Half a crown, and sixpence for the man.'
Leon Molin: front, a chemist's shop.
The room beyond seemed subterranean:
Oblique light from a garden, fishtank green.

The sharp, specific foreignness of things:
Floor-standing ashtrays, chromium-plated shrubs
With hungry bulbous roots; bright flasks of 'spray';
Loose stacks of *Titbits*, *Picture Post*, *Reveille*;
A hatstand with more coats than customers.

Waiting my turn, I'd try to calculate
Which one I'd get: the white-haired on the left,
A kindly grandfather I'd never known,
Or the smart schoolmasterly bully on the right,
Glancing at me archly: 'Next, young man!'

At home, my father sometimes washed my hair
In glutinous amber shampoo: 'Soup!' he'd call,
As my dripping scalp emerged from its solution
Of Nucta Oil, brand from the gullible past,
Like Kolynos toothpaste, verdant chlorophyl –

Obtainable, no doubt, from Leon Molin.
Yet I'll retain my vexed embarrassment
At one shy boy's charade of confidence,
And two old barbers, threatening and mild,
Meekly accepting pennies from a child.

Allotments at Baldock

Spilled out beyond the gasworks and the railway,
Scattered at random on the injured ground,
They lie, detached extensions of elsewhere,
Like amputated artificial limbs.

Potatoes, peas, broad beans, mad cabbages,
Eccentric uncut flowers which bloom to seed
Seek the embankment's gritty sanctuary
Or reappear among surprised back-yards.

On unclaimed plots, an uninvited rash
Of poppies and, in crowded insolence,
Massed nettles, elder, hogweed, clematis
Proclaim a little civilisation's end.

From land-locked beach-huts, corrugated sheds,
Come sounds which seem obscurely nautical,
Marine metallic tinklings, and sad flags
To frighten off the doubtful inland birds.

Thus signalled is a patchwork of possession,
A borrowing unmortgaged, a free space
Devoutly Sunday-tended, reaffirming
Our weedy and tenacious-flowering grace.

Working

For you, that summer, working was a need:
Shirtless, you shovelled rubble, hacked through wood,
Reclaimed a fireplace swathed in age and soot.
A sandstorm of brick-dust settled in your sweat.

So, like a manic god, you changed my world:
Hands textured like burnt bark, flesh torn and mauled
From work's compulsions. Later I'd begin
To learn the gentler touch of that rough skin.

You've Changed

I looked, of course, across a crowded bar,
Admired at once the perfect sense of poise,
Deep chestnut eyes, abruptly squared-off jaw
Which made you so much more than pretty. Days

Passed uncounted, months, and maybe years
Until that Sunday evening when I saw
You sitting at a table in the garden,
Dalton's Weekly and a drink beside you.

'You look like something out of Graham Greene,'
I said absurdly, meaning I suppose
You had the air of an expatriate.
I might have put it otherwise: 'You've changed.'

Immeasurable the distance that can pass
Across a glass, and then another glass:
The truths and reckless confidence exchanged
As a long evening grows to over-late.

No real surprise to see the cracks appear.
We knew them all along: the tear, the scar
Which makes us so much more than perfect, through
A lifetime spent on books and booze and boys,

On things that were, or even things that are.

The Difference

We watch the gathering dusk through sepia dusk
Across a beach of fish-heads, glass beads, relics
Dumped by a careless deity called chance.
Ferry and trawler exchange a passing glance.

Dark comes fast: lighthouse and streetlamp pierce it.
You sit at the window, silent as I write.
We are no longer locked in self-defence.
Being with you has made all the difference.

Providence

The Providence Baptist Chapel, Aldringham,
Is light industrial: factory for souls,
Abandoned among heather, fern, and gorse,
Where birches lean their leaves against the wind,
It prompts old questions. Why here? Why at all?
I half-admire that monstrous confidence,
Unthinking certainty of doing good,
Which dumped a bumptious bright-red-pantiled barn
Out here, far from community and road.
Now broken-windowed, boarded and patrolled
(It says) by ghostly guard-dogs, Providence
Has fallen out of use.
                                    Young oaks surprise
And jostle through the rusted graveyard fence.
The loyal congregation, being dead –
Adah Cadey, Sam Studd, Jabez Bird –
Worship in green, while yellow daisies dance
Upon the grave of Percy Marjoram,
Tended with love's defiance.
                                    I walk on,
Along a sandy track, a silent lane:
New planting, like a wartime cemetery
Or rockets poised for launch on Guy Fawkes' Night,
Proclaims the future forest's greener hope;
And a neat brick row of charitable homes
Shows how goodwill can be inhabited
As peace of mind, as warmth.
                                    Yet faith runs cold.
A sign outside the Baptist Chapel said:
'Black Horse Agencies (Subject to Contract) SOLD.'

Yaxley

Last time here, I'd have been too small to walk,
When Freddy displayed his derelict retreat,
The Old School House (now renamed after him);
My grandmother, his devoted Tiggywinkle,
Benignly at ease in the big sloping fields.

And I can see why he'd have liked the place,
How the ancestral village touched his puritan soul;
While the vast airy spaces spoke of liberation,
His thatched hedgy corner offered sanctuary.
He craved, like all great artists, a modest nest.

Yet what am I doing, with notebook and camera,
Expecting the terror of dim recognition?
A trackless bridge, cow-parsley, distant traffic,
Cemented parish pump...but, beyond all this,
A scent on the air of the summer still to come.

Two Rollerskaters in Oakley Square

Like evening gnats these adolescents find
    An island of late sunlight
To turn and circle in, and to unwind
    Their tangled day to night.

The dark plump one makes his agility
    Appear a conjuring trick:
A purple sphere, it's marvellous that he
    Can twist and spin and flick

His ankles over pavement-edge or grating;
    Ends vindicate his means.
Beyond, his friend comes, slyly hesitating
    In faded sawn-off jeans,

Bleached spiky hair, precisely ripened tan,
    Wide-striding sinewy grace:
He wears his body almost like a man,
    Choosing new movements, new pace.

A Year or Three

· 1: 1987

It's the end of a year: strange to feel that
In frosty March. Season of birthdays –
All these lives a numeral older: it

Shouldn't surprise us to find the calendar's wrong.
Spring holds fire, undefined; shy daffodils
Wear crisp, frost-bitten edges; and the long

Haul of a winter shifts to second gear.
At last I know again that we'll not baulk
The final gradient: now all's in store,

Contained potential like an actor's breath,
Withholding utterance for the given cue,
Preparing to turn action into myth.

The cue's there, though the script for your first night
May not have been the text you had in mind,
Nor this the poem which you said I'd write.

The dry-cleaner's son is ruining my life.
Two years ago, he'd help out Saturdays,
Slight boyish chores rewarded with ice-cream.

Last summer he'd grown lanky, self-aware:
Out in the street, washing his father's van,
They staged a grand balletic water-fight.

Now, taller of the two, he calls me 'mate',
Will deputise for dad, or join him in
A loose bravado, male confederacy.

His shirts – today, gigantic hippie flowers –
Are as loud as his crotch-line; and his former selves
Lost postcards of the summers left behind.

3: 1991

Late June. The steady, stately dance of rain;
Abandoned Test and washed-out Wimbledon;
And thus the dreadful summers start again.

A ragged starling, like a cartoon chick,
Panics on the sill in futile search
For crumbs that my tame blackbird may have missed.

Reminds me of the sixties: songs of sun
And surf while, racked with adolescence, we
Observed the world through sheets of summer rain.

(We cheered in '66, Election Night:
'We'll never see the Tories in again.'
How wrong we were and, in a way, how right.)

Is history's motif no more than this?
Wet summers and another era's end,
Diminuendo, faltering reprise?

Perhaps: a charm to call old summers in
As evidence, as silent witnesses.
The years are dying. *Fin de siècle. Fin.*

III

The Lunatics' Compartment

A Courtly Epistle for A.J.

It's England, nineteen eighty eight.
The rain comes on, the train comes late.
I choose the lunatics' compartment:
In front, a snow-thatched don, intent
On squinting back across his seat;
Behind, protruding trainered feet,
A stoned recumbent boy, half-dressed,
Prompts academic interest.

At Finsbury Park, the spiral stairs
Are urinous as ever; there's
The rumble of the train I've missed;
Two Irishmen, already pissed,
Dispute the time. Three stations on,
A grinning beefy lad sits down:
His left leg pressed on my right, he
Checks out desire's seismology.

Next into Thresher's at Earl's Court,
Seeking the dry white I'd want brought
To my own party. Outside, it's
Time to give thanks for leather jackets:
I sprint off down the rain-surged street,
Pass John Heath-Stubbs and know we'll meet
In Redcliffe Gardens, think about
Just one in the Coleherne? Better not.

Inside the hall, we greet and kiss.
You say, 'We don't usually do this
When we meet in London.' And that's so,
But here it's suddenly as though
We're self-enclosed if not alone.
A naked boy is on the phone,
And from an open door drift through
Camp music and a voice or two.

The room's embalmed from nineteen ten:
Old furniture, old books, old men,
And now an odd perception, which is
Candles here have dimmer switches.
The wine is white and warm and sweet,
The chatter joylessly discreet;
No intellectual risks are taken
Until…of course, it's Eddie Linden.

Enters mid-sentence, going on
About getting mugged in Paddington,
Which makes him now, amazingly,
Sober and plastered, as if he
Is London: walking-wounded place
Whose gracefulness is in disgrace,
Whose refugees are gathered here,
The brave and literate and queer.

The naked boy, now dressed, is an
Escapee from the Barbican:
He looks around this courtly scene,
Unsure but every inch a queen,
Creating little waves of truth
As each of us recalls his youth
Or wonders who will take the plunge
And make some sad nostalgic lunge.

Elsewhere Hugh David talks about
The English Gentleman, that lout
On whom he's writing; Francis King
Decides to tango, though nothing
Seems (luckily) to come of it;
And I remember Michael Schmidt
At Earl's Court Square: 'We're getting old:
You've grown eyebrows, I've gone bald.'

It's not my scene, I guess, and so
At ten o'clock I turn to go:
I use as my excuse a train,
Though feel the pull of bars and rain.
A cinematic staircase kiss
Brings its lovely echo, this:
The poem, not our love, is finished;
I would not have that love diminished.

Strangeways

'Hooded rioters, a noose hanging from a pillar, appeared on
the roof yesterday with a possible hostage. The man's hands
are bound, and he seems to be being threatened with a
carving knife.'

Caption in The Independent, 4 April 1990

Those hooded gestures look familiar
From mutilated statues, gargoyles,
Dark icons of forgotten underworlds.
The fork is from the cutlery of hell,
Portending some slow medieval death.
One pallid central figure clasps bound hands
In slack, uncertain attitude of prayer:
His level gaze is sculpted as a mask,
His arms bulked out of all proportion,
Carved limbs upon an aristocratic tomb.
They stand, the three of them, against scarred arches;
Another lurks beyond the churchly pillars,
Attending to a noose.
                      This is our time:
Each culture gets the myths that it deserves.

True Stories

A Little Rain or Drizzle

Sun, you see: sun's unreality
Flooding the smudged surfaces of life.
All's reinvented, clean; but there may be
A little rain or drizzle before dusk.

Poetry Society

Tonight an evening for the little poets,
There being no big poets left alive.
The reader carries a speech impediment,
The chairman a handbag. I'm wondering
How to persuade the peanuts along the bar.

Base Boys

They lounge around the share-a-ride layby
Like almost ordinarily aimless lads,
Ill-fitted in their clothes, yet can't disguise
Bad haircuts, shiny features, nervous eyes.
This grid of buildings, service roads could be
A campus: University of War.
They learn jokes here: 'Why's Saddam Hussein
Like a pair of tights?' 'They both' –
The unblushing answer – 'irritate Bush.'
The School of Politics is strong
On economy of language. 'Man,' he says,
'We're going to *concrete* Iraq.'

Michael Laskey on a Bicycle

Hatted and scarfed as a red Christmas card,
He pedals down Main Street, like in a movie,
Because in Leiston, it has to be said,
There's nothing you could call seriously High.

How Are You Today?

Dear Peter Barker: I could take
The progress of roses with Patricia Hughes;
Tom Crowe's mistakes; or even Donald Price
Declining to read a story in the news.
But what the waking soul cannot endure is:
'This is Peter Barker opening up
Radio 3, *and how are you today?*'

Look

Just one look, just like the song,
That's all it took, and here I am again,
Anguishing by my Anglepoise lamp again,
Waiting for open bars, open arms, open.

Yoggit

They call him Yoggit, because he says,
'I always has yoggit for me tea.'
Watches the fight, then shadow-boxes,
Punching grey air. 'Go on, Yoggit.'
He dances, punishes the empty space,
Sees shadows, but these pensioners are real.

Neil's Yard

It's anarchy out there: nicotiana
Stoned out of their flowery heads;
Ivy-leaved pelargoniums
Gone woodily assertive; and beans,
Up the wall, over the roof…

It's hard to keep up: I rescue fronds
Of lolling Chilean glory vine
(And end of course by snapping them);
Winged purple bells downturned,
Fuchsias in suspended mid-dive…

And then the welcome invaders:
Poppies, toadflax, yellow vetch,
Lobelia – all self-seeded hangers-on…
A boudoir for bees, an aphids' banquet:
What god of paradox has made this place?

Crane-flies and Dragon-flies

September, and the coastal insect life
Is reinvented by Heath Robinson:
Crane-flies dangle by spare limbs from webs
Or land on sand to drown in the next wave;
Above the abandoned railway-track inland,
Bright dragon-flies like airshow prototypes
Fly stunts among the berries, fading blooms.

King's Cross

There are things which I cannot determine, even on good days.
Why is the open-door-button a breast in a mortuary?
How did today's ticket sneak to the back of my wallet?
Why do I always end up in the lunatics' coach?

Mr Gadget

Today he's mending Emma's typewriter,
And tinkering with another vintage car,
While planning his next essay on aesthetics
(Holding ideas up in his hands like bricks).

Tonight he'll lurk, webbed in his special corner,
And contemplate the boys along the bar;
His dreams are coated with procrastination
(It's just an act of the imagination).

Gulls

'Boat ashore 3.30 – 4 pm.'
These seawise birds know better:
The clamorous mob escorts it in,
Sharper than starlings, hardly gullible.

Inland

The summer's burden turns to benediction.
Softened by sudden warmth, the leaves relax
And rest upon the breeze. We should have known
That this was what we wanted all along.

A Photograph of Thomas Mann

You remember the one.
It's on the backs of 50's Penguins.

The pen's held at an angle of thought:
Or second-thought, proof-correction.

The mouth's a mere line of contained
Amusement, self-deprecation.

And the veined warty face tells of age,
Its age: when writers

Wore sombre spectacles, bankers' suits,
And dignity, and hope.

George

I'd say no pub's complete without its George –
Crabby, cantankerous, in a corner near the bar.
One was stone-deaf, looked like Sibelius;
Another had his own stool, bottle, glass;
But only you were Irish too. So when
An overdressed woman's pampered poodle trod
On your foot, you growled: 'You fucking stupid bitch.'
'He isn't,' she snapped primly, 'he's a dog.'
'I wasn't,' you said, 'referring to the dog,'
And rearranged the contours of your face,
Sniffing a bit, yet radiant with gin.

The Gift

All we have is all we have to say,
Unless the gift becomes a giveaway.

Citrus

If required to devise a desirable addiction,
    I would choose citrus.

Orange-juice, grapefruit coax the hungover soul
    To zestful good humour.

A messy selection of kitchen ingredients
    Is chastened by lemon.

Shades from pale lime to overripe orange
    Make waking worthwhile.

My desert island needs not only discs
    But these fruitful spheres.

Aubergines

After hours, off-duty, the young chef talks:
He perches, in his denim earnestness,
On a bar-stool, folds himself like an omelette,
And worries about his troubles with aubergines.

There are times to be not a fly on the wall,
Nor in the soup, but a kind ironic god:
Invisible, I watch the two of you press on
Through the whole ratatouille of emotion.

Moving House

'This is a dream,' I tell myself, waking,
'And what it says isn't real.' But there's my house,
Its stairs and its ramshackle rooms overflowing
With people from the street, and that blonde girl you knew.

I've really no idea what they're all doing there,
This whole vacant parade of the unwanted world.
Now we've found our own space, so I no longer care:
Released from your wrapping, you are my present.

Yet what subtle adjustments we've made since we began
To know each other last winter: I've even grown to love
Those dead flattened vowels you claim as Australian.
Holding you now, I could tear you apart like bread.

My head on your musky chest, I must have slept,
Waking to find the house still crowded, its furniture
Dispersed and rearranged, all out of place except
You, warm in weak sunlight on your nest of denim.

I cautiously explore: a pine table from the kitchen
Is wedged into the study, whose papers and books
Are strewn in the bathroom, my history rewritten
By strangers who view me with unconcerned reserve.

And here's the blonde girl, perched on the landing,
Leaning on a sideboard I've never seen before.
'I told you he wasn't like that,' she says, smiling.
'Oh, but' – I'm smiling too – 'he is. He is.'

Editorial

1

Don't go on about the hell
Of creation: analyse;
Make a pattern; learn to spell.

2

Last night's manuscripts depress:
Choose, today, a typewriter
With a prepossessing face.

3

Discard your drafts; yet store them,
Coffee-stained and torn, for they
Await your variorium.

Their Silences

I am shocked, now, by their silences:
The poets whose blurbs, twenty years ago,
I enviously scanned. Where are they now?

Did marriage, mortgage and a family
Intrude between them and the clean white page?
Did common sense extinguish all their rage,

And leave them common, sensible? I know,
As rain, a leaking gutter's metronome
Ticks off the minutes, urgencies of home,

The jobs not done, the bills not paid, and so
I curse that smug complacent ancient fool
Who dared to say my life was comfortable.

Poet and Cat

i.m. Fritz (*aka Fishcat, Fishcake, Fishkas*)
d. 16 September 1993

No doubt it's the subject of some aspiring PhD:
    If so, you'd better be
In there among the longer footnotes, Fishcat.
    Inimitable from that
Original head-through-window brisk self-introduction,
    You soon settled on
Our working relationship: I worked, you related;
    At least, you tolerated
First-draft furies from your chair near my desk, wheezing
    A bit, then sighing
With paws-over-ears resignation and a silly tabby grin.
    Some days, when I'd let you in,
A whole North Sea gale behind you, you'd land with the noise
    Of squashed teddy-bear toys;
Once mauled by a gull, scared of anything with wings,
    You'd chunter at starlings,
But happily tackle dogs, adults, over-attentive children;
    Rebuked too often
By a sniff and flick of tail, I'd got your food fads known
    Better than my own.
Indestructible eccentric, how could you do this to me?
    Buried at sea:
Fit end for an Aldeburgh beach-cat, if end there had to be.

Poet and Robin

R.B.F. 1912-1991

The aged poet prods his compost-heap,
Reminded of a former jest that he
Might make a decent mulch eventually,
For as you sow (he thinks) so shall you reap.
He wonders at the odd longevity
Not just of turnip, say, or cabbage-stalk,
But of hydrangea's mop-head levity.
A robin watches from his garden-fork,
With sly ironic glance, who seemingly
Approves and even shares the poet's mood,
Or humours him as harbinger of food.
The other thinks of how unerringly
All compost turns afresh, on its own terms,
To flower and fruit; to poets, robins, worms.

IV

In Another Light

Not even sun's false innocence
Can cover this: smaller today,
The island finds its boundaries,
Flexes as the tide subsides
And waves bathe other surfaces.

I share the land's astonishment
At the beach's lowered profile:
Planed to pebble-smoothness,
Uneasy in its changed shape,
It mutters, rattles, settles.

Gulls discover new salt lakes
Among the silent, stoic cows;
Beyond the damp seaweedy sand
Which marks the ocean's last advance,
The shingle ridge has rolled inland.

The surge spent, in another light
Storm dwindles into memory,
And children from the local school
Scatter the debris of the night,
Revising their geography.

Hundred River

We came to Hundred River through a slow October,
    when earth is scented with everybody's past;
when late scabbed blackberries harden into devil's scars,
    untasted apples rot to bitter toffee.

Across reed-beds a track of blackened railway-sleepers,
    a plank-bridge lapped by barely-stirring water;
swans gargling silently in their fine indifference;
    above, a sky of urgent discursive geese.

Now the year has turned again and I am alone here,
    where willow-herb's dry white whiskers drift over
the brick-red spikes of sorrel and the gossiping reeds;
    and the river sullen, muddied after rain.

No movement in the woods but stealthy growth of fungus,
    hesitant leaf-drop, distant scuttle of deer:
in one marbled, stained oak-leaf I sense gigantic change,
    and in the drizzle feel the season fracture.

A Virus

The words won't scan. Initials, acronyms
Are tidier though no less threatening:
They claim it for bureaucracy, as if
Depriving it of an imaginary life.

I try: I sense it crazily adrift
On a wild surge of involuntary current,
Like the lost boat in a forgotten nursery rhyme.
It had no choice in the matter, meant no harm.

But see how it turns our calm world upside-down!
Your comical pill-popping hypochondria
Seems mere rehearsal for reality,
Your lithe past an irrational vanity.

So now your boast is: 'Look, I've put on weight.'
Your breakfasting on booze has given way
To healthy muesli, yoghurt, wholemeal bread,
Storing up strength for the wasted days ahead.

The Reasonable Shore

And there are days, beyond dog-days of summer,
When the restless ocean gathers in repose,
Soughing and lapping at unprinted sand,
Proving that greatest power is power contained.

Shakespeare's shore of reason was the mind
Which, he believed, the tide would cleanse and fill
With water's bright lucidity. How could
A dark intelligence hold such faith in good?

The mirror-sea, example and reproach,
In each return confounds the cankered past
And leaves a world renewed with each withdrawal
(Though that is not what Shakespeare meant at all).

Sailing Home

You know I always loathed the gang of them.
Two days at sea, already quarrelsome,
They squabble over titles, territory,
As if that mattered: their minds mutiny.
Meanwhile at least a kindly wind assists us;
The sky, as brittle-sharp as Venice glass,
Is cloudless; and the low late-autumn sun
Patterns the deck with shadow. An old man,
I sit here writing, unmissed, undisturbed
And (I confess) not wholly discontented:
My life at last's resolved, my long task ended,
As from the start I'd cunningly intended.
Strange, all the same, this interrupted cruise
To win back what I hadn't grieved to lose
And shan't know what to do with when we reach
The thriving port and populated beach:
An old world full of cares, affairs of state.
The point of islands is they're isolate.

But there's my daughter: thinks she's royalty,
Looks forward to it, even may enjoy
A life of plots and power, of bugs and spies,
Grand gestures and expensive ceremonies.
I wish her well: or hope that food and wine
May recompense her for the asinine
Attentions of ambassadors and princes,
Bewigged buffoons and daisy-headed dunces.
Some have a taste for politics; but some
(Alas, such as myself) are overcome
By an urge to find in words the hint of meaning,
Whereas the courtly crew use them for preening –
The clause a comb, the phrase a powder-puff –
To prettify thin air, give form to fluff.

Of course, I could have stayed. You think so? No.
Not just because an end's ordained, although
It fell together like a perfect cadence,
But more because I'd outworn that pretence.
A man can't live surrounded by his errors:
I tried to civilise, to tame the terrors
Of things by nature nurtureless, untamed;
Where even sun and moon had been unnamed,
And every word rebounded as a curse,
As bad as courtly flummery, or worse!

There's no solution, then: maybe that's why,
Out here between dark sea and fading sky,
I feel this strange suspended happiness:
Things may go wrong, but things are more or less
For once beyond my meddlesome requests.
So, no more island shipwrecks, no more tempests.
When I get 'home', I'll treat the eye and ear,
Catch up with Caravaggio, and hear
What Monteverdi's written in my absence:
Who knows, perhaps there'll be a new Renaissance.
I've much to learn, and much more to forget
In my long autumn afternoon; and yet…

Before I lost my art, I saw the future:
How greed would feed on greed, and war on war;
Though man may learn to conquer pain, disease
Will deviously mutate. So death or madness
Must overtake the race, the failing planet.
And, worse, I came to see that this was right,
The globe's sole hope of greenness and rebirth,
Replenishing a grey, smoke-shrouded earth.
No states to govern, none to educate:
Do birds imagine? Butterflies create?
They are their art: have no need to invent
These foolish forms through which we represent

Our second-bestness. You of course will know
All this already, knew it long ago,
And yet...I almost said 'One last command',
Forgetting that I'd left you on our island.
The dusk draws on: I'm talking to the stars.
Perhaps, my absent friend, I always was.

The Stones on Thorpeness Beach

For Guy Gladwell

O luminosity of chance!
Light spins among the spider-plants
As sand or amber glow seeps through
Tall windows of a studio,
While on the beach in random rows
The enigmatic stones compose
A silent staveless variation,
The music of regeneration.

Re-learn astonishment, and see
Where splinters of eternity
Still glitter at the water's edge,
Beyond the tideline's daily dredge
Of flotsam: plants and creatures who'd
Survive this stale decaying world,
And stones worn smooth as solid tears,
Each crafted by a million years.

Or dusky rain across the sea,
Dull pewter light, when suddenly
The level sun breaks through, makes clear
Another perfect hemisphere:
Its rainbow-self, supported by
A dark horizon, arcs the sky.
I watch the colours falter and,
Slipping on shingle, fall on sand.

Yet, high above the crumbling cliff,
A concrete pill-box stands as if
In crazy gesture of defence;
As if the huge indifference
Of change, decay, might somehow be
Perturbed by such small dignity
Which slowly shifts and cracks, and so
Will shatter on the stones below.

Search for a sound hypothesis:
'Safe as houses', 'Bank on this',
Dead clichés of security!
Houses? Bank? You'd better tie
Mementoes in a plastic bag,
Chuck in the sea, mark with a flag
The spot where fish or mermen may,
With luck, remember you some day.

Our rented time is running out,
But unlike tide won't turn about
With regular and prompt dispatch
To land upon the beach fresh catch,
As gradually, with gathering pace,
Life ebbs out from the human race
Inhabiting a world grown ill.
Time for a benediction still:

Peace to the gulls and guillemots,
To curlews and their bleak mudflats,
To sea-birds, sea-anemones,
To marsh-plants, meadow-butterflies,
To lavender and gorse and mallows,
To creatures of the depths and shallows;
Peace to the vast blue out-of-reach,
Peace to the stones on Thorpeness Beach.